The BIG MEETING

Story by **Oliver DeMille**
Illustrated by **Eric Hungerford**
Original Characters by **Chris Brady**

Copyright © 2015 by LIFE Leadership

All rights reserved. No part of this book may be reproduced or transmitted in any form or by any means, electronic or mechanical, including photocopying and recording, or by any information storage and retrieval system, without the written permission of Obstaclés Press. Inquiries should be sent to the publisher.

Obstaclés Press and the Obstaclés logo are trademarks of LIFE Leadership.

First Edition, May 2015

10 9 8 7 6 5 4 3 2 1

Published by:

Obstaclés Press
200 Commonwealth Court
Cary, NC 27511

lifeleadership.com

ISBN: 978-0-9961843-0-4

Illustrated by Eric Hungerford

Printed in the United States of America

He stayed in bed even after he woke up, groggily trying to figure out what was wrong.

Rascal loved these trips with his Mom and Dad to big conventions. First, it allowed him to spend time with his best friend, Lance, even though they lived in West Virginia.

TODAY SHOULD BE FUN. I'M GOING TO WATCH A MOVIE WITH LANCE AND KAYLA!

SMART!

Second, he really liked teasing Kayla. She wasn't like most girls around his age. She was... He struggled for the right word.

That word didn't do her justice, but it was a start.

That did it for Rascal. He knew that the slimy mean guy was just trying to lie to him like he lied to the others, but Rascal knew for sure that he trusted his dad. If he was supposed to stop talking, so be it.

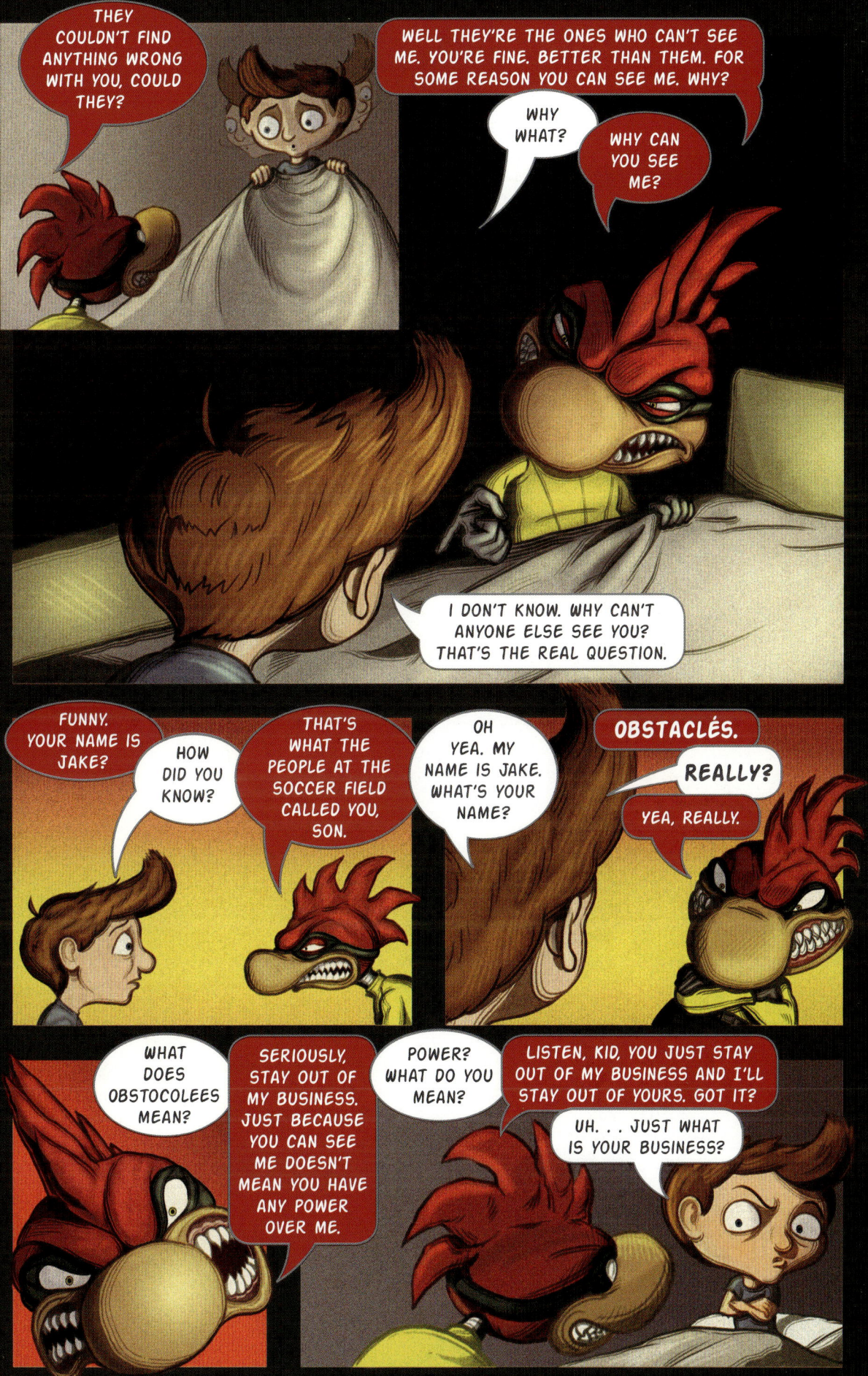

MAYBE I MADE THE WRONG CHOICE. OR MAYBE OBSTACLÉS JUST DOESN'T KNOW I'M IN MILWAUKEE.

WHO IS OBSTACLÉS?

UH, NOBODY. I WAS JUST THINKING TO MYSELF.

ARE YOU EXCITED ABOUT SEEING LANCE TODAY? OR ARE YOU MORE EXCITED TO SEE HIS LITTLE SISTER KAYLA?

BIFF

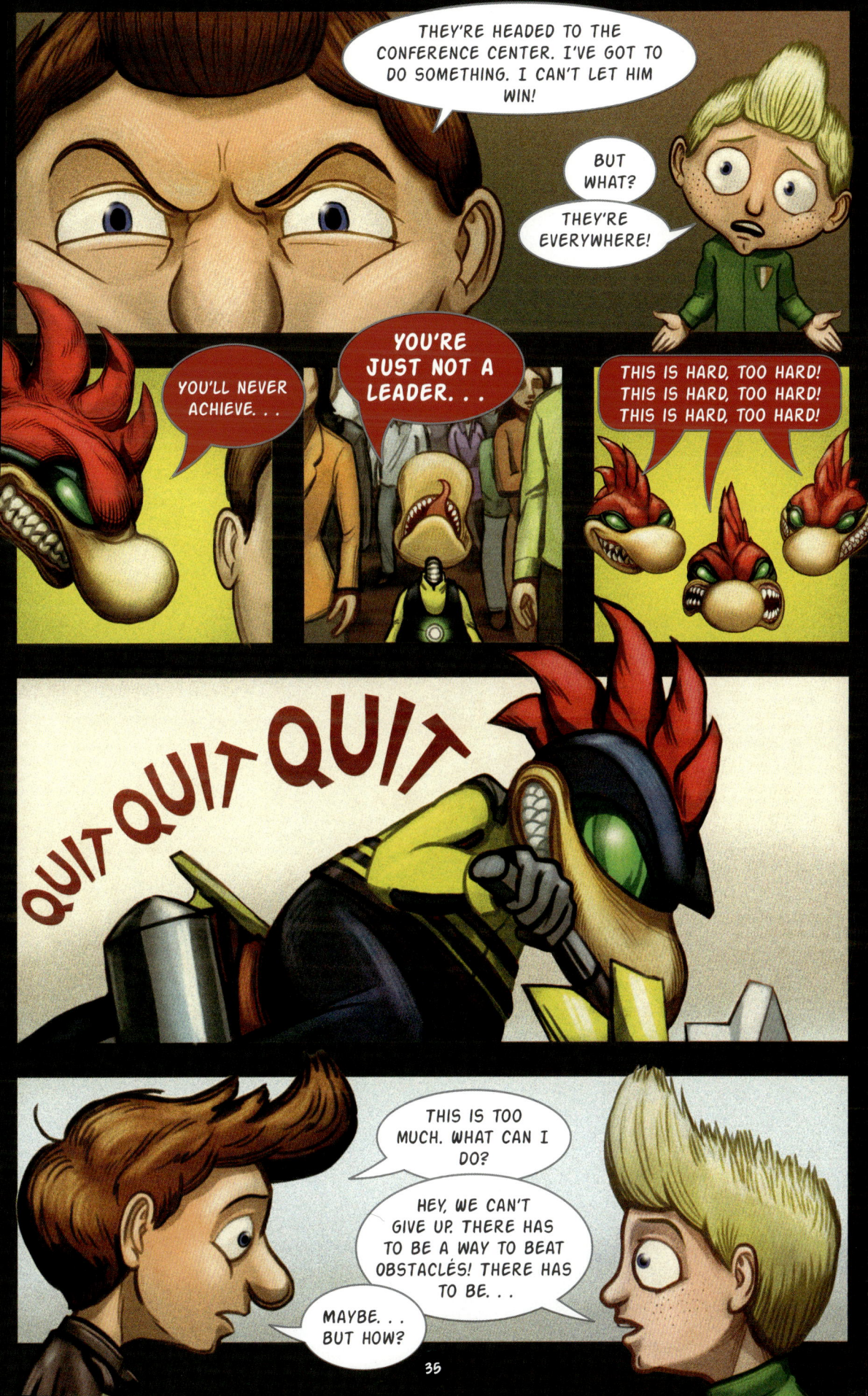

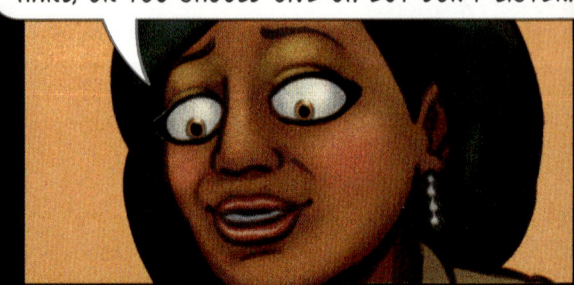

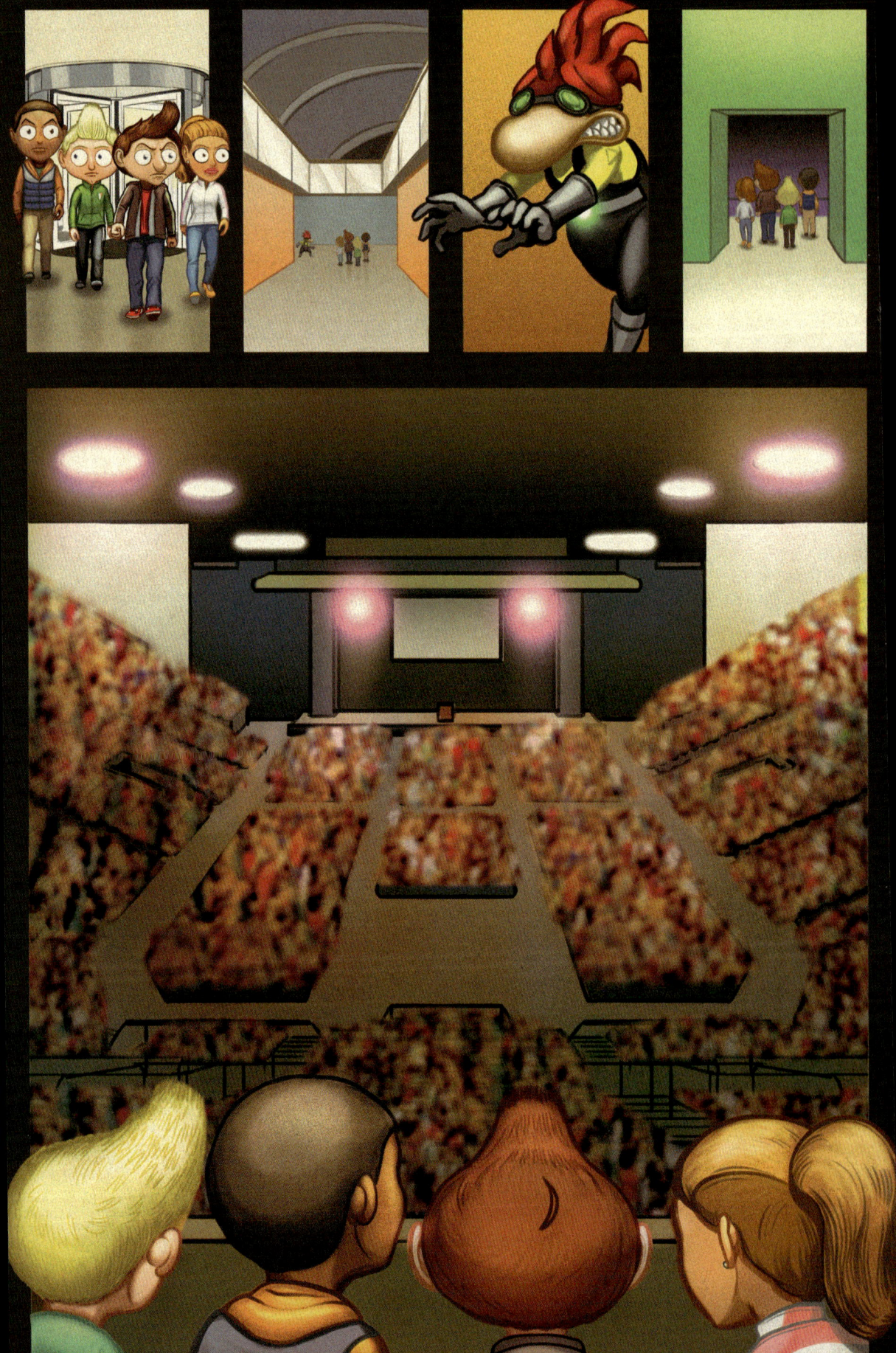